STAR WARS

ROGUE ONE™

DEATH STAR

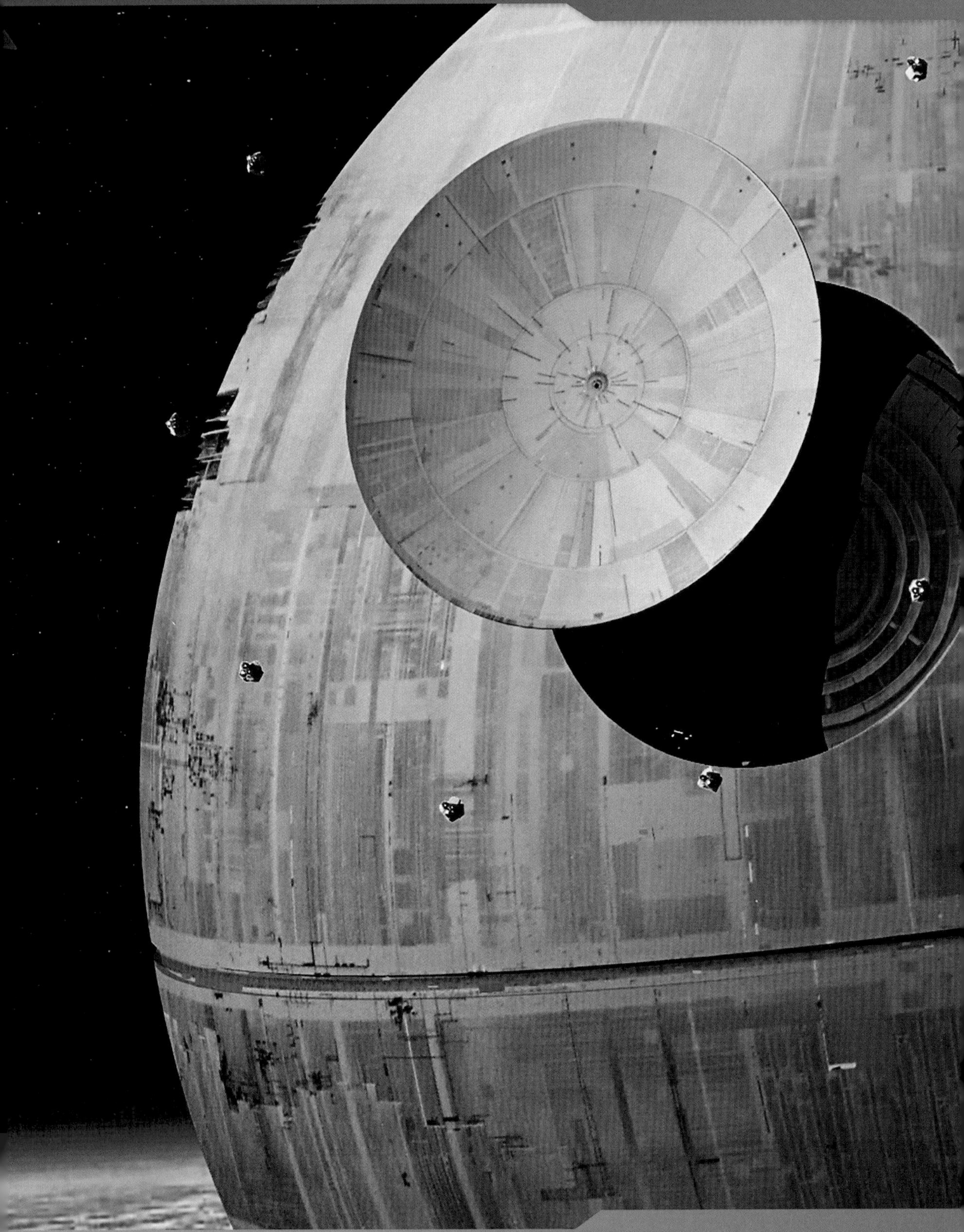

STAR WARS

ROGUE ONE™

DEATH STAR

Inside the Formidable Battle Station

BY RYDER WINDHAM

INCREDI BUILDS®

A Division of Insight Editions, LP
San Rafael, California

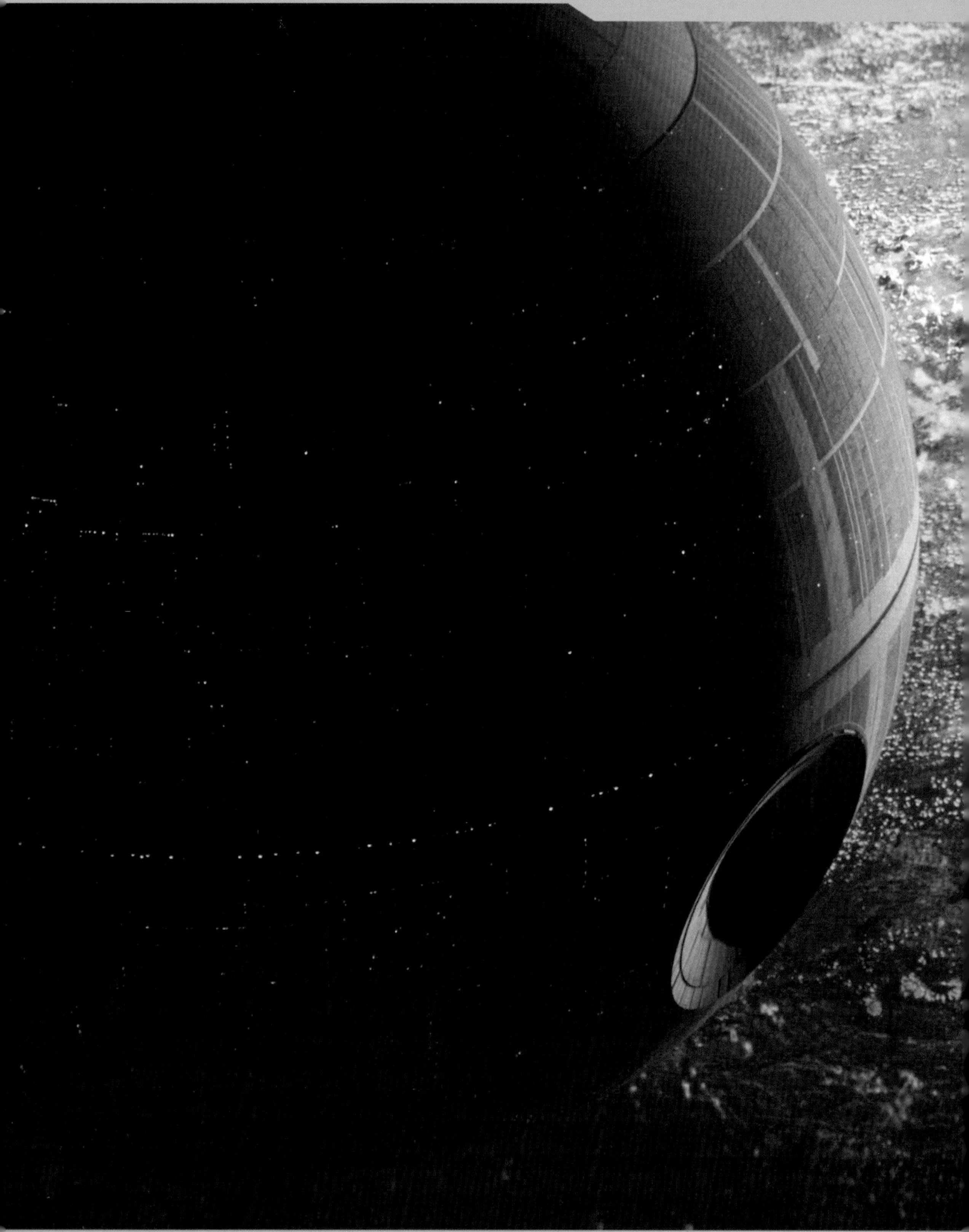

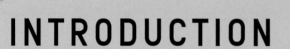

INTRODUCTION

After Supreme Chancellor Palpatine undermined the Galactic Republic, decimated the noble Jedi Order, and declared himself Emperor, the Sith Lord needed to ensure that every planet in the galaxy would bow to his rule. In order to achieve this end, Palpatine created "the ultimate weapon," an enormous, spherical battle station equipped with a superlaser capable of destroying a planet with a single blast: the Death Star. Palpatine believed this "technological terror" would make all his opponents fear him, and would therefore enable him to expand his control over the galaxy. However, one of the key minds behind the Death Star, scientist Galen Erso, secretly built a critical design flaw into the battle station that allowed the Empire's main opposition, the Rebel Alliance, to destroy it.

Three years later, the Emperor unveiled a second, more powerful Death Star, which he planned to use to destroy the entire rebel fleet. Although engineered to prevent the same catastrophe that claimed its predecessor, the second battle station was still under construction and not as impenetrable as Palpatine believed. Blinded by his own hubris, the Emperor failed to foresee that the second Death Star would also be destroyed by the rebels, shortly after his own death at the hands of Darth Vader.

To some, the Death Star became a symbol of terrifying technology. To others, it was the last vestige of Imperial glory. Eventually, a new regime called the First Order would embrace Imperial ideals as well as nightmarish scientific advances to create a next-generation superweapon that would cause the stars to tremble. Even thirty years after the destruction of Palpatine's second battle station, the Death Star's malign influence continues to haunt those who seek to restore freedom to the galaxy.

DEATH STAR

At the time of its construction, the first Death Star was the largest object ever built. Despite its immense size, the battle station was equipped with a hyperdrive, enabling travel through hyperspace to nearly every star system in the galaxy.

TECHNICAL SPECIFICATIONS

MANUFACTURER: Imperial Advanced Weapons Research

CLASS: Space battle station

DIAMETER: 160 kilometers

WEAPONRY: 1 superlaser, 15,000 turbolaser batteries, 2,500 laser cannons, 2,500 ion cannons, and 768 tractor-beam emplacements

SHIELDS: Equipped

HYPERDRIVE: Class 4; backup unit Class 20

LIFE SUPPORT SYSTEMS: Equipped

CREW: Mission dependent, service roster ranges from 1,186,295 to 1,206,293

CARGO CAPACITY: Over one million kilotons

CONSUMABLES: 3 years

ALDERAAN'S END

Grand Moff Tarkin, the Imperial military leader in command of the Death Star, wanted citizens of the galaxy—especially members of the Rebel Alliance, which opposed Imperial rule—to know that the battle station was fully operational. When rebel leader Princess Leia Organa of the planet Alderaan attempted to deceive Tarkin with false information about the location of the rebels' secret base, Tarkin responded by firing the station's superlaser at her defenseless homeworld. The planet was destroyed instantly.

SUPERLASER

The Death Star's primary weapon was a massive superlaser, which was clearly visible as a broad concavity—approximately 38.5 kilometers in diameter—on the battle station's upper hemisphere. Eight initiator laser cannons ringed the concavity's circumference and fired beams that converged to form a single, powerful beam. The combined energy in that single beam carried more firepower than half of the Imperial fleet, and was capable of blasting an entire planet into space dust.

EQUATORIAL TRENCH

From a distance, the Death Star's equatorial trench resembled a dark band that wrapped around the battle station. The trench held docking bays and weapons emplacements, and was connected to other trenches that intersected at right angles across the station's surface. Imperial engineers programmed every trench's defensive systems to prevent turbolaser batteries from accidentally blasting each other or damaging the station's hull.

DESIGN ORIGINS AND SECRET DEVELOPMENT

Before the birth of the Empire, the Sith Lord Darth Sidious instructed his apprentice, Count Dooku, to contract engineers on the planet Geonosis to create the first designs for an enormous spherical battle station. The Geonosian engineers drew inspiration from structural configurations and technologies used in Neimoidian Trade Federation warships to design the moon-sized Death Star.

TRADE FEDERATION BATTLESHIP

To threaten opposing worlds and gain greater control over trade routes throughout Republic space, the Trade Federation transformed its fleet of Lucrehulk-class cargo freighters into battleships. Each battleship was over three kilometers in diameter and resembled a flattened disc forming a split ring around a central sphere. The ring, which previously housed cargo holds, carried Trade Federation droid starfighters. The sphere contained the ship's massive computer and a compact hypermatter-annihilation reactor.

TRADE FEDERATION CORE SHIP

The Neimoidians converted their battleships' central spheres into detachable core ships, which were engineered for planetary landings and equipped with land and air defenses. Each core ship was 696 meters in diameter. The Trade Federation used its core ships and battleships throughout the Clone Wars.

HOLOGRAPHIC PLANS

On the planet Geonosis, Geonosian engineers manufactured battle droids and weapons for the Trade Federation. Count Dooku, the leader of the Separatists and a former Jedi, persuaded the Geonosians to join the Separatists and break away from Republic rules and regulations. Dooku also commissioned the Geonosians to supply him with holographic plans for the "ultimate weapon."

SITH LORD SCHEME

On the planet Coruscant, Count Dooku delivered the secret plans to his Master, the Sith Lord Darth Sidious, known to the masses by another identity: Supreme Chancellor Palpatine, leader of the Galactic Republic. The plans for the ultimate weapon were vital to the Sith Lord's scheme to conquer the galaxy.

IMPERIAL LEADERS

Although many Imperial subjects, slave laborers, and droids participated in the construction of the Death Star, four individuals were instrumental in overseeing its completion.

THE EMPEROR

A former Senator of the planet Naboo, Sheev Palpatine was secretly the Sith Lord Darth Sidious, and used the dark side of the Force and political maneuverings to become the leader of the Republic. Palpatine orchestrated the Clone Wars, and it was during this conflict that he first began planning construction of the Death Star.

DARTH VADER

Once a Jedi named Anakin Skywalker, Darth Vader betrayed his fellow Jedi to become Palpatine's Sith Lord apprentice. After a duel with his former Jedi Master, Obi-Wan Kenobi, left Vader close to death, the Emperor reconstructed Vader as a cyborg. On the Death Star, Vader served as the Emperor's representative. Vader had nothing but disdain for the Imperial officers who believed that the Death Star was more powerful than the dark side of the Force.

GRAND MOFF TARKIN

A veteran of the Clone Wars and one of the Emperor's most loyal administrators, Grand Moff Wilhuff Tarkin rose rapidly through the ranks of Palpatine's newly formed Empire. Palpatine put Tarkin in command of the Death Star, which Tarkin championed as a means to crush all dissent to Imperial rule.

DIRECTOR ORSON KRENNIC

A native of the planet Lexrul, Orson Krennic rose through the ranks of the Galactic Empire and was eventually promoted to Director of Advanced Weapons Research. Krennic's primary directive was to complete the Death Star and deliver it to the Emperor.

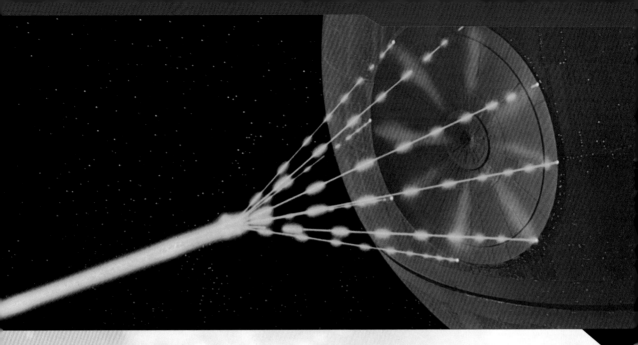

CONSTRUCTION

ANNIHILATION

Working from Geonosian plans for a deep-space battle station, the Empire began the secret construction of the Death Star in orbit around the planet Geonosis. Numerous challenges, including the lack of a functional superlaser, led to ongoing delays for the project's completion. After the Imperial Security Bureau realized a rebel agent was investigating Imperial activities in the Geonosis system, the Empire used biological warfare technology to exterminate billions of Geonosians before relocating the construction project to deep space in an effort to keep the project a secret.

SUPERLASER

To accelerate progress on the Death Star's super-laser, Orson Krennic coerced scientist Galen Erso into researching kyber crystal dynamics. Imperial technicians and engineers worked from Erso's data to build the final functional superlaser on the planet Eadu. Imperial forces then transported the enormous kyber crystal-based weapon to the Death Star, fitted it into the battle station's superstructure, and connected it to the station's hypermatter reactor.

THE FATE OF THE HOLY CITY

As the Empire hurried to complete the Death Star, Grand Moff Tarkin ordered Director Krennic to conduct a fractional test of the Death Star's superlaser on the city of NiJedha, capital of the small desert moon of Jedha, which was once important to followers of the Force. Even a small portion of the superlaser's total reactor yield was sufficient to devastate the entire city and surrounding territory. To keep the Death Star project secret, the Empire spread word that the city was devastated by a cataclysmic mining accident.

DEFENSES

TURBOLASER TOWERS

Turbolasers carry destructive power sufficient to punch through energy shields and armored plating, and are the primary defense against enemy warships and starfighters. The Death Star was blistered with thousands of towers that supported twin turret-mounted turbolaser cannons, which could rotate in a full circle. Gunners were stationed in chambers at the base of the towers, beneath the battle station's surface, and relied on sensors to aim at incoming targets.

LASER CANNONS

Capable of destroying an enemy starfighter with a single shot, manned Super Blaster 920 laser cannons were linked to tactical computer systems throughout the Death Star, and had a faster recharge rate than most cannons. Each cannon required a crew of three: a standing gunner, a seated targeting technician, and a seated energy technician. Death Star gunners wore specialized computer helmets to assist with tracking fast-moving enemy targets. The gunners were stationed in pressurized chambers with open ports that were protected by invisible energy shields, similar to those used in docking bays.

TRACTOR BEAMS

A standard feature on starships, tractor-beam projectors emit invisible, maneuverable force fields that can capture, shift, or redirect objects. The Death Star's crew used tractor beams to guide Imperial starships in and out of hangars and docking bays, and also to snare enemy vessels. After the Imperials captured the Corellian freighter that carried the Jedi Master Obi-Wan Kenobi and his allies Luke Skywalker, Han Solo, and Chewbacca, Kenobi stealthily infiltrated the station's central core to deactivate Tractor Beam 12 and allow his friends to escape.

TIE FIGHTERS

The Death Star carried thousands of Imperial TIE (twin ion engine) fighters, highly maneuverable short-range combat ships. TIEs were built without energy shields and hyperdrive engines so that all their power could be directed toward weapons and propulsion systems. The single-pilot cockpit was bracketed by a pair of solar-collector wings that drew additional power from surrounding stars. Darth Vader piloted his own bent-wing TIE prototype to defend the Death Star during the attack by rebel starfighters that ultimately led to the battle station's destruction.

INSIDE THE DEATH STAR

DOCKING BAYS

The Death Star's surface and equatorial trench was lined with numerous docking bays and hangars of various sizes. These bays accommodated scores of Imperial shuttles, fighter crafts, and maintenance vessels. Docking bay entrances were lined with energy shields that separated and protected the bays' pressurized interiors from the vacuum of space, and decks were illuminated with directional markings to guide ships to safe landing areas. Openings in the decks housed lifts to deliver troops and maintenance crews from lower levels. To ensure safety and prevent stowaways from invading and sabotaging the battle station, Imperial scanning crews used sophisticated sensors to search starships for life-forms, weapons, and explosives.

TURBOLIFTS

To convey Imperial personnel to different areas within the Death Star, multi-directional turbolifts traveled through a vast network of crisscrossing cylindrical shafts and tubes that linked every sector in the battle station. Turbolifts were positioned in clusters every few hundred meters on each floor level, leaving at least one turbolift readily available at any given cluster. Despite the speed and efficiency of the turbolift system, Imperial personnel sometimes found it more expedient to circumnavigate the Death Star via shuttle, flying directly from one docking bay to another.

DETENTION BLOCKS

Accessible by turbolifts, the Death Star's detention blocks were located far from the battle station's main command areas. Their long corridors were lined with cells featuring bare metal walls and magnetically locking doors. Imperial wardens stationed in detention block control rooms used sophisticated surveillance equipment to monitor prisoners and prevent escapes. To further discourage captives from rebelling, detention block walls held laser traps—built-in automatic weapons that could fire at non-Imperial personnel.

TRASH COMPACTOR

The Death Star's rooms and corridors had trash disposal chutes that led to large waste collection bins and trash compactors. The compactors were engineered with metal walls that moved toward each other to crush trash to the smallest possible size. After liberating Princess Leia from a Death Star detention block, Luke Skywalker and his allies became temporarily trapped within a compactor. Along with assorted garbage and waste materials, the compactor also contained a dianoga, a creature notorious for slipping into spaceport sewers and starship bilges.

MILITARY PERSONNEL AND DROIDS

STORMTROOPERS

After the Clone Wars, Emperor Palpatine assigned the Grand Army of the Republic's clone soldiers to serve as Imperial stormtroopers, and also bolstered and eventually replaced their ranks with enlisted non-clone volunteers. Like their Republic predecessors, the Empire's foot soldiers are clad from head to toe in white armor that is resistant to most projectile weapons and blast shrapnel. Their armored suits also have built-in temperature controls that enable them to endure a range of environments. On the Death Star, stormtroopers were armed with blaster rifles and wore utility belts that carried additional weapons and tools for fighting insurgents.

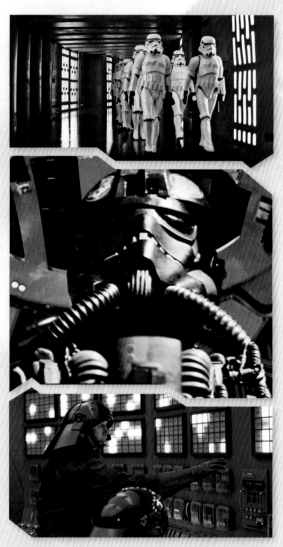

TIE FIGHTER PILOTS

An elite class of the Imperial military forces, TIE fighter pilots wear pressure-sealed flight suits with chest armor that features a control box for life-support systems. All the TIE pilots who served on the Death Star trained for months in simulators to learn flight tactics, gunnery, and deep-space navigation. The simulators also tested the pilots' reflexes and stamina, preparing them to act and react without hesitation during combat missions. Because TIE fighters lack energy shields and hyperdrives—thereby limiting their pilots' chances for survival or any option to escape—TIE pilots are highly motivated to pursue and destroy their targets quickly and with incredible precision.

DEATH STAR TROOPERS

Wearing black uniforms and flared, reflective helmets, high-ranking Death Star troopers were stationed on the battle station's Overbridge. They monitored data and issued orders from their command sector duty posts, piloted the battle station to its destinations, and—following direct orders from Grand Moff Tarkin and his generals—initiated the firing sequence for the superlaser.

DEATH STAR GUNNERS

The Death Star carried two contingents of Death Star gunners. The first manned the laser cannons that lined the defenses along the Death Star's trenches. The second group was a more elite force, which worked in conjunction with Death Star troopers to operate the superlaser. Both contingents of Death Star gunners wore specialized computer helmets equipped with sensor arrays to assist with targeting.

INTERROGATOR DROID

Engineered by the Imperial Department of Military Research and used by the Imperial Security Bureau, the model IT-0 interrogator droid is programmed to torture and obtain information from enemies of the Empire. To achieve its goals, the IT-0 wields a hypodermic syringe that dispenses a variety of chemicals that stimulate cooperation. A low-power repulsor enables the droid to hover above the floor so it can move around its victims easily. The IT-0 is also equipped with an electroshock assembly and sonic torture device.

MOUSE DROID

Designed and manufactured by Rebaxan Columni, the MSE-6-series droid—commonly known as a mouse droid—is a longtime mainstay on starships, a roving repair robot that also carries messages and cleans floors. Each mouse droid travels on four driver wheels, and magnetic links enable the droids to connect and travel in tandem. On the Death Star, mouse droid duties included guiding troops through corridors to their assigned posts. A command order tray located on top of the droid held sealed orders that were protected by security access codes.

DEATH STAR DROIDS

Manufactured by Arakyd Industries, RA-7 protocol droids typically serve as translators and data analysts, and have been in production since before the Clone Wars. The Empire commissioned Arakyd to produce thousands of RA-7s as personal servants for Imperial officers on the Death Star. Because RA-7s were fairly ubiquitous on the battle station, Imperial crews nicknamed these protocol units "Death Star droids."

REBEL ASSAULT

ALLIANCE INTRIGUE

When Rebel Alliance leader Mon Mothma learned that the Empire was constructing a secret super-weapon, she conscripted streetwise Jyn Erso, the daughter of Galen Erso, to discover more about the project. With the help of Alliance intelligence officer Cassian Andor, former Guardians of the Whills Chirrut Îmwe and Baze Malbus, defected Imperial pilot Bodhi Rook, and reprogrammed Imperial droid K-2SO, Jyn led a mission to steal the plans to the battle station. Their daring raid would strike a blow against the Empire that would be felt throughout the galaxy.

R2-D2'S MISSION

After rebel agents transmitted the Death Star plans to Princess Leia's starship, Darth Vader and his stormtroopers captured Leia's ship in orbit over the desert planet Tatooine. Realizing she couldn't escape, Leia instructed the astromech droid R2-D2 to deliver the plans and also a recording—a personal plea for help from Jedi Master Obi-Wan Kenobi.

BATTLE PLAN

With the help of Luke Skywalker and his allies, R2-D2 eventually delivered the Death Star's technical readouts to the Rebel Alliance's secret base on the moon Yavin 4. After rebel technicians analyzed the data, they located the weakness built into the design by Galen Erso: an unshielded, two-meter-wide thermal exhaust port—a small opening to a shaft that traveled straight to the Death Star's hypermatter reactor system. The rebels concluded that firing proton torpedoes into the exhaust port could cause a chain reaction that would destroy the entire battle station. The rebels had to act fast because the Imperials had set the Death Star on a course for Yavin 4 with the intention of destroying the entire planet.

THERMAL EXHAUST PORT

The Death Star's surface featured numerous exhaust ports that released excess thermal energy from the battle station's hypermatter reactor. The rebel pilots' target was an exhaust port located in a trench near the top of the station's upper hemisphere. Because the exhaust port was small and defended by Imperial laser cannons, some pilots thought that firing proton torpedoes directly into it would be impossible. However, Luke Skywalker was confident they could hit the target because he had previously bulls-eyed womp rats—which were about the same size as the exhaust port—while flying his T-16 skyhopper back home on Tatooine.

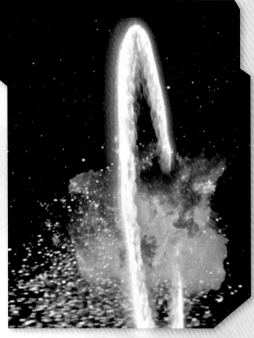

TRENCH RUN

Flying in X-wing and Y-wing starfighters, rebel pilots skimmed the Death Star's surface and descended into the battle station's trenches to evade Imperial turbolasers. Darth Vader ordered the deployment of TIE fighters for ship-to-ship combat, but when he realized the rebels were trying to reach a vulnerable exhaust port, he boarded his own TIE fighter and joined the fray. Flanked by two wingmen, Vader veered into a trench and opened fire on the rebel fighters.

MASSIVE EXPLOSION

The rebels had already failed at two attempts to hit their target when Grand Moff Tarkin commanded the Death Star gunners to use the superlaser on Yavin 4. But before the superlaser could fire, Luke Skywalker managed to launch two proton torpedoes directly into the exhaust port. Just as the rebel technicians had predicted, the torpedoes caused a series of energy backlashes that traveled to the battle station's main reactor. Skywalker and his allies raced away from the Death Star mere seconds before it ruptured and exploded. Grand Moff Tarkin perished in the blast, but Darth Vader escaped to fight another day.

DEATH STAR II

The Rebel Alliance would later discover that the Emperor commissioned a more advanced battle station, which the Imperials constructed in the remote Endor system. The second Death Star was equipped with a faster hyperdrive and a more sophisticated superlaser, which was capable of blasting relatively small moving targets, such as enemy starships, as well as obliterating entire worlds.

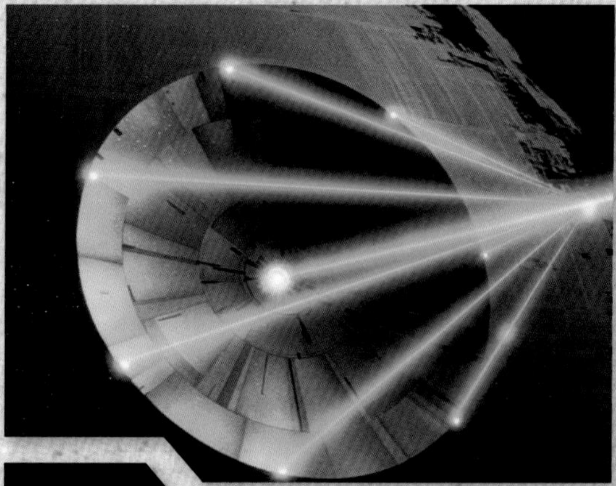

TECHNICAL SPECIFICATIONS

MANUFACTURER: Imperial Advanced Weapons Research

CLASS: Space battle station

DIAMETER: 200 kilometers

WEAPONRY: 1 superlaser, 15,000 turbolaser batteries, 15,000 heavy turbolasers, 7,500 laser cannons, 5,000 ion cannons, and 768 tractor-beam emplacements

SHIELDS: Equipped

HYPERDRIVE: Not yet equipped

LIFE SUPPORT SYSTEMS: Equipped

CREW: Unknown; based on estimates from original service, roster ranges from 1,186,295 to 1,206,293

CARGO CAPACITY: (When completed) over one million kilotons

CONSUMABLES: (When completed) 3 years

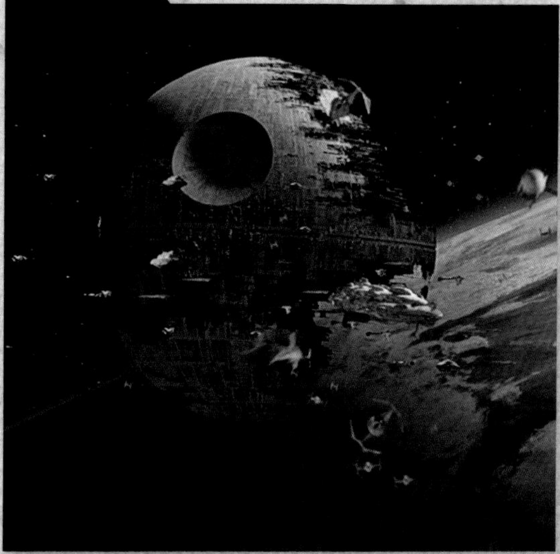

THE EMPEROR'S TRAP

The second Death Star was still under construction in orbit around Endor's forest moon when the Emperor deliberately leaked false data about the battle station. Just as the Emperor expected, the rebels soon obtained and analyzed the data, and determined that the unfinished station could be vulnerable to an attack. The rebels scrambled their warships to the Endor system, but quickly realized that the Emperor had lured them into a trap—the second Death Star's energy shields, hypermatter reactor, and superlaser were fully operational!

PLANETARY SHIELD GENERATOR

Although Imperial star destroyers guarded the second Death
Star's orbital construction site, the battle station's most
important defense was a planetary shield generator located
on the surface of the forest moon of Endor. The towering
shield generator projected an invisible energy shield around
Death Star II, protecting it from concussion missiles, aster-
oids, comet strikes, and enemy warships of any size. A rebel
strike team traveled to the forest moon in a desperate effort
to destroy the shield generator, which would allow their allies
to pilot starfighters into Death Star II's superstructure.

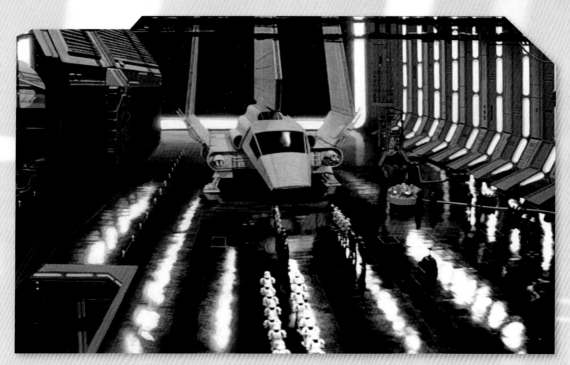

INSIDE DEATH STAR II

EXECUTIVE DOCKING BAY

Located within Death Star II's equatorial trench, the executive docking bays were reserved for high-ranking Imperial officers and dignitaries, and were more heavily fortified than docking bays used for standard transports. Imperial engineers constructed the largest executive docking bay for Emperor Palpatine, and positioned it near a smaller bay reserved for Darth Vader. Both bays could accommodate arrivals and departures of Imperial Lambda-class shuttles. Imperial regulations required all person-nel within the docking bays to stand at attention when officials disembarked and boarded executive vessels.

EMPEROR'S THRONE ROOM

Perched at the top level of a high tower on the Death Star II's northern pole, the Imperial throne room was housed within an armored chamber and served as Palpatine's private command center for every sector of the battle station. Dedicated ener-gy-shield generators and projectors ensured that the throne room was the station's most heavily defended location. The tower housed a turbolift for access to the throne room, which was further protected by laser traps and rotating squads of stormtroopers and the Imperial Royal Guard.

SUPERSTRUCTURE TUNNELS

A large opening in the unfinished surface of the second Death Star allowed access to the battle station's superstructure for construction and maintenance vehicles. After rebel troops destroyed the planetary shield generator that protected the station, rebel pilots were able to fly their ships into the station's access tunnels in order to target the station's reactor core.

HYPERMATTER REACTOR

Located deep within the center of the second Death Star, the hypermatter reactor powered all systems on the battle station, including the superlaser, turbolaser emplacements, hyper-drive generators, and life-support systems. More sophisticated than the reactor in the first Death Star, this reactor had numerous subsystems and defenses to prevent enemy proton torpedoes from being fired through ventilation shafts to reach the reactor's core. However, after the rebels destroyed the shield projector that protected the Death Star, nothing prevented rebel pilots from flying their own starfighters into the shafts that led to the reactor and firing torpedoes at the structure, setting off a chain reaction that would destroy the battle station.

STARKILLER BASE

After the Rebel Alliance defeated the Empire at the Battle of Endor, the Alliance founded the New Republic and dismantled the Empire's military apparatus. However, a new and malignant force known as the First Order arose from the ashes of the Empire to spread terror and oppression throughout the galaxy. Thirty years after the destruction of the second Death Star, the First Order unleashed an even more destructive super-weapon: Starkiller Base.

ADVANCED TECHNOLOGY

The First Order used all its resources to transform an ice planet dotted with forests into Starkiller Base, a mobile battle station. Although Starkiller Base retained the planet's naturally spherical shape and possessed an enormous, circular muzzle that echoed a Death Star's super-laser concavity, its resemblance to the Death Star was largely superficial. Instead of drawing power from a man-made hypermatter reactor, Starkiller Base harvested energy from the planet's nearest star and then converted that energy into an ultra-powerful beam that could blast through hyperspace and destroy multiple worlds in distant star systems with a single shot.

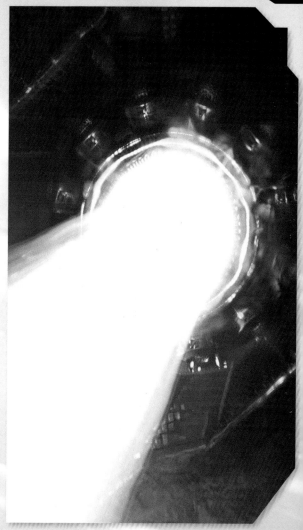

BASE DEFENSES

During its construction, Starkiller Base was one of the First Order's greatest secrets, as well as the key to its plan to conquer the galaxy. The First Order defended its base with powerful planetary shields, TIE fighters, and missile and laser batteries, as well as legions of stormtroopers, snowtroopers, armored walkers, and ancillary sentry and patrol droids.

GENERAL HUX

The son of an Imperial Academy commandant who fled to the Unknown Regions, General Armitage Hux grew up hearing the legends of how the Empire had defeated the Jedi and won the Clone Wars. As the commander of Starkiller Base, Hux believed the New Republic was too weak to maintain political stability, and that only the First Order could save the galaxy. Hux also revived Grand Moff Tarkin's Imperial ideal: achieve military superiority through technological terror. Despite the First Order's safeguards, a determined resistance strike team disabled and destroyed Starkiller Base's thermal oscillator, which destabilized the planet's core and caused the entire superweapon to implode. Hux was among the Imperials who escaped the massive explosion.

BEHIND-THE-SCENES

CONCEPT ART

Ralph McQuarrie was the first artist that director George Lucas hired for *Star Wars: A New Hope*, the first *Star Wars* film. McQuarrie's credentials included detailed technical illustrations for Boeing and animated sequences of the Apollo space missions for NASA and CBS News. He visualized Lucas's ideas for *A New Hope* in a series of concept sketches and paintings, and his renderings of the Death Star's surface, trenches, interiors, and occupants served as a foundation for model makers, set designers, special effects artists, and costume designers.

A Ralph McQuarrie concept for *Return of the Jedi* shows two Death Stars under construction.

DEATH STAR REDESIGN

Artists initially rendered the Death Star's superlaser so it was centered over the sphere's equator, but George Lucas decided to reposition the laser above the equator. Because Lucas's revised instruction came too late for computer animator Larry Cuba to change his work on the Death Star plans that appear on screen during the rebel pilots' mission briefing, the plans look slightly different from the Death Star model.

The miniature Death Star is prepped for filming a sequence in *Star Wars: A New Hope.*

DURABLE DEATH STAR

Model makers in Lucasfilm's special effects department, Industrial Light & Magic (ILM), joined two three-foot-diameter Plexiglass domes to form a globe for the Death Star model. They created the "laser crater" by cutting a hole in the globe, flipping the convex remnant, and positioning it in the hole so it appeared as a concavity. The model's surface required thousands of pinpricks to allow an internal light to shine through, creating the illusion of windows and navigational lights for the space station. When ILM moved its California operations from Van Nuys to San Rafael in 1978, it inadvertently threw away the Death Star model. Fortunately, the model survived mostly intact and is now part of a private collection.

DELICATE DEATH STAR

Like the first Death Star, the superweapon featured in *Return of the Jedi* began with two Plexiglass domes that model makers joined together. To make the Death Star look as if it were under construction, model makers removed parts of the surface and inserted layers of etched brass to create an exposed superstructure of miniature girders. However, the model's inner frame wasn't reinforced with steel or aluminum, and the brass pieces were so fragile that they were susceptible to sagging over time. Today, this Death Star model does not travel on museum tours due to its delicate state and is currently housed in the Skywalker Ranch Archives.

SETS

For *A New Hope*, production designer John Barry contracted a company to produce plastic panels for the walls of the Death Star interior sets. According to Barry, the set pieces could be assembled and reconfigured in "endless ways," allowing the movie's crew to reuse the pieces for multiple locations, including the Death Star's corridors, hangar bay, and detention block.

VISUAL EFFECTS

Before the advent of computer-generated visual effects, filmmakers relied on traditional techniques and ingenuity to bring certain shots to the screen. For the battle sequence over the Death Star in *A New Hope*, model makers created a large "wall" to represent the battle station's surface. To film explosions and the close passes of starfighters flying over the Death Star's surface, ILM cameraman Richard Edlund operated a VistaVision camera while seated on a moving pickup truck in the ILM parking lot.

DEATH STAR CAMEOS

When George Lucas needed to shoot a pair of Death Star technicians at a control board, *A New Hope* concept and storyboard artist Joe Johnston and model maker Jon Erland donned costumes and acted out the firing of the superlaser.

The highly detailed miniature of the second Death Star created for *Return of the Jedi*.

The visual effects crew on *Star Wars: A New Hope* use a truck to capture shots of explosions on the Death Star's surface.

INTERVIEW WITH DOUG CHIANG

After graduating from the film program at the University of California, Los Angeles (UCLA), Doug Chiang worked as an animator on *Pee Wee's Playhouse* and directed television commercials. In 1989, he began working as a visual effects art director at Industrial Light & Magic (ILM). Subsequently, he became the design director for *Star Wars: The Phantom Menace*, concept design supervisor for *Star Wars: Attack of the Clones*, and a concept artist on *Star Wars: The Force Awakens*. He currently serves as Lucasfilm's vice president and creative director for *Star Wars*, and oversees *Star Wars* films, games, and theme parks. As production designer for *Rogue One: A Star Wars Story*, his duties included working with director Gareth Edwards to recreate the Death Star that first appeared in *Star Wars: A New Hope*.

On *The Phantom Menace* and *Attack of the Clones*, you created vehicles that were retroactively based on the Death Star. Did you feel you were already steeped in Death Star design before you started working on *Rogue One*?

Yes! When I started working with George Lucas on *The Phantom Menace*, he was very adamant that we actually create a design history so that all the designs would eventually make sense with all six films [in the first two *Star Wars* tril-

ogies]. And so we decided that the Empire was going to have very graphic geometric shapes, and a ball, a sphere, was going to be one of those iconic images. That kind of permeated the design philosophy. When you see the ball at the center of the Trade Federation battleship, it kind of foreshadows the Death Star. And I love when visual design can draw all those connections that the audience then starts to see. You know, how designs evolved and how they became what they are now.

Do you remember the first time you saw the Death Star in *Star Wars: A New Hope* (1977) and concept artist Ralph McQuarrie's production paintings—his early concepts of the Death Star—for that film?

Yes, I remember that very well because I learned how to design and paint by studying Ralph's work. I was fifteen at the time. When his portfolio paintings came out, I was really drawn to how he depicted those forms, and the Death Star was one of them. It was the way he captured the scale from a simple ball because if you think about it, a ball is really hard to determine scale. It could be the size of a marble or the size of a planet. And what Ralph did was build in all these visual tricks and surface details, and other little elements that really kind of informed the sheer scale of it. [He layered] in all these levels of details so that, as you approached the Death Star, more details and more surprises were revealed.

How did you go about creating new exterior views of the Death Star for *Rogue One*?
The original Death Star was a model, and the close-ups were all matte paintings. We collected all the visual evidence, including all the original concept paintings by Ralph McQuarrie, and we created our own hybrid, but stayed true to the design itself. For example, the Death Star that you see in *A New Hope*, you don't really see the north and south poles, but in *Rogue One*, we wanted to see those new angles. That begged the question, what do the north and south poles look like? We went back and looked at some of Ralph's paintings, where he sketched some of those ideas. And even though those views hadn't been seen on screen before, we wanted to be faithful to the spirit of Ralph's original design. From there, it was a matter of updating all the materials for scale and dramatic purposes. Our effort was to convince audiences that they were seeing the original model from new points of view.

For *A New Hope*, the Death Star's interior sets consisted of modular walls and panels that could be reconfigured for various rooms and corridors, and also utilized 1970s-era control panels and switches. Were the Death Star sets similar for *Rogue One*?
Yes, absolutely. We actually built ours to the plans that were originally drawn. We didn't want to depart from that, in terms of the old-fashioned switches and buttons. We wanted to keep that very true. In fact, a lot of the keyboards you see in *Rogue One* stay true to what was available in the 1970s. But we did make some upgrades. For example, in *A New Hope*, if you look at the wall behind Obi-Wan and Darth Vader during their duel, you'll notice that the pillar lights are all kind of warped because of the heat from the light sources. We knew that we didn't want to recreate that hallway exactly, so we made the walls with sturdier material that wouldn't warp under the heat. Our approach was that we took the spirit of the design but updated the way it was manufactured.

Did you create new interior and exterior areas of the Death Star that audiences haven't seen before?
Yes and no. We had contemplated designing—and we actually designed—sets of different areas of the Death Star. It was ultimately decided that we would stay with the iconic because we didn't have that many story moments within the Death Star itself. We thought it was very important that when we went into the Death Star we would actually see familiar locations, and so we saw things like the control room. At one point we were seriously playing with the idea that we might revisit the conference room but unfortunately that didn't play out in the story.

How does Gareth Edwards's direction style and his general creativity differ from George Lucas's, and what do they have in common?
It's interesting. Both of them are heavily steeped in documentary filmmaking styles. George's favorite filmmaking style is documentary films and Gareth definitely comes from that too. And one of the things that drew me to Gareth was that his filmmaking style was a very handheld documentary look. And that was the philosophy that he used to approach this film: to make it feel real like a documentary filmmaker was shooting this version of the movie on the *Star Wars* set. And what that demanded was we needed to design and build the sets with freedom for Gareth to find the shot on the day. Typically, when I was working with George, he was very specific. When we presented the set model of what we wanted to build, he'd say, "No, I'm going to shoot this scene into these two walls. All you have to do is build those two walls." Gareth, on the other hand, was like that but he also said, "Give me the other two walls as well because when I'm in there that day I might find a really good shot, and that will allow me to turnaround." And so our big challenge for *Rogue One* was that we had to build the sets in full 360 where possible, and by doing that, Gareth was able to find moments and great compositions that we totally couldn't have anticipated.

MAKE IT YOUR OWN

One of the great things about IncrediBuilds™ models is that each one is completely customizable. The untreated natural wood can be decorated with paints, pencils, pens, beads, sequins—the list goes on and on!

Before you start building and decorating your model, choose a theme and make a plan. You can create a replica of the dreaded Death Star, or you can make something completely different. Anything goes! Read through this sample project to get you started and those creative juices flowing.

DEATH STAR REPLICA

WHAT YOU NEED:
- Gray and black paint
- Paintbrush
- Sharpened pencil

WHAT YOU MIGHT WANT:
- Mechanical pencil

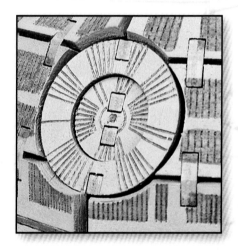

STEPS:

1. Start by painting the Death Star with a thin coat of gray paint.

2. Mix some black paint into your gray paint to make it a shade or two darker. Mix in a little water to thin the paint out.

3. Using the darker shade of gray, paint the engraved areas on the models. Let dry.

4. Use a finely sharpened pencil—or a mechanical one— to emphasize the engraved lines.

5. To finish, paint the stand black.

It will be easier to craft the Death Star with the model mostly assembled, but the stand detached.

IncrediBuilds™
A Division of Insight Editions, LP
PO Box 3088
San Rafael, CA 94912
www.incredi-builds.com
www.insighteditions.com

 Find us on Facebook: www.facebook.com/InsightEditions
 Follow us on Twitter: @insighteditions

Library of Congress Cataloging-in-Publication Data available.

ISBN: 978-1-68298-097-2

Publisher: Raoul Goff
Art Director: Chrissy Kwasnik
Designer: Yousef Ghorbani
Executive Editor: Vanessa Lopez
Managing Editor: Alan Kaplan
Project Editor: Chris Prince
Production Editor: Lauren LePera
Editorial Assistant: Hilary VandenBroek
Associate Production Manager: Sam Taylor
Product Development Manager: Rebekah Piatte
Model Designer: Liang Tujian, TeamGreen

For Lucasfilm
VP Creative Director at Lucasfilm: Doug Chiang
Editor: Sammy Holland
Creative Director of Publishing: Michael Siglain
Story Group: Leland Chee, Matt Martin, Pablo Hidalgo
LFL Asset team: Newell Todd, Travis Murray, Bryce Pinkos, Erik Sanchez

Insight Editions would like to thank Angela Ontiveros and Danny Saeva.

Insight Editions, in association with Roots of Peace, will plant two trees for each tree used in the manufacturing of this book. Roots of Peace is an internationally renowned humanitarian organization dedicated to eradicating land mines worldwide and converting war-torn lands into productive farms and wildlife habitats. Roots of Peace will plant two million fruit and nut trees in Afghanistan and provide farmers there with the skills and support necessary for sustainable land use.

Manufactured in China by Insight Editions
10 9 8 7 6 5 4 3 2

SOURCES

Hidalgo, Pablo. Star Wars: *The Force Awakens: The Visual Dictionary*. New York: Dorling Kindersley, 2015.

Rinzler, Jonathan. *The Making of The Empire Strikes Back*. New York: Del Rey, Ballantine Books, 2010.

Windham, Ryder. *Star Wars: Imperial Death Star Owner's Workshop Manual*. Somerset, UK: Haynes Publishing, 2013.

Windham, Ryder. *Star Wars: The Ultimate Visual Guide*. New York: Dorling Kindersley, 2012.

ABOUT THE AUTHOR

RYDER WINDHAM's credits include over seventy *Star Wars* and Indiana Jones books. An advocate of voluntary blood donations, he encourages *Star Wars* fans and all eligible donors to give blood regularly.